Bird-Watching Do's . . . and

P9-DHS-767

Do only go to places you know are safe.

Do be respectful of birds, nature, and other bird-watchers.

Do sit quietly and move slowly.

Do try to be inconspicuous, and try to blend in with the scenery.

Do try to be friendly to other bird-watchers! They are generally a pretty nice bunch of people.

Do be patient! You might not identify every bird that comes along, and that's all right. Every time you go out, you'll learn a little more.

Do give birds their space!

Do check for ticks when you get home!

Don't put yourself in harm's way, ever!

I could climb up there, easy! It's not so steep!

It's only a bird. Really.

Don't ever frighten or bother parent birds and their babies.

Just a little closer...

Hello—police?

Don't go into peoples' yards without their permission.

KEEP OFF DUNES

BIRD NESTING AREA

Dee dee dee

Don't pretend you didn't see those signs.

This is not a cormorant

This is not a hawk.

Don't be fooled by this plastic bag and this grocery cart.

Don't sit on poison ivy.

Don't tread on delicate plants.

Do not do this. I don't care who you are following.

It is quite impolite.

CHESTERFIELD COUNTY PUBLIC LIBRARY
CHESTERFIELD, VA

For Dave and James

Copyright © 2013 by Annette LeBlanc Cate

All rights reserved. No part of this book may be reproduced, transmitted, or stored in an information retrieval system in any form or by any means, graphic, electronic, or mechanical, including photocopying, taping, and recording, without prior written permission from the publisher.

First edition 2013

Library of Congress Catalog Card Number 2012942416
ISBN 978-0-7636-4561-8

12 13 14 15 16 17 LEO 10 9 8 7 6 5 4 3 2 1

Printed in Heshan, Guangdong, China

This book was typeset in Sabon.
The illustrations were done in ink and watercolor.

Candlewick Press
99 Dover Street
Somerville, Massachusetts 02144

visit us at www.candlewick.com

You usually see me at the beach!

You might see me in a city!

So many great birds around...

We're everywhere!

Look Up!

Bird-Watching in Your Own Backyard

Annette LeBlanc Cate

Me, I wouldn't be caught dead in a backyard.

Unless there was dead stuff in it, of course.

What's this "look up" business? Why not "look down" once in a while?

with special technical assistance from Jim Barton

CANDLEWICK PRESS

During the preparation and proofing of this book, I benefited from the technical assistance of Jim Barton from Cambridge, Massachusetts, a veteran birder with forty-five years of experience. For many years, Jim has led field trips and taught bird identification for the Boston office of the Massachusetts Audubon Society, the Friends of the Mount Auburn Cemetery, the Cambridge public schools, and the Brookline Bird Club.

Contents

I'm gonna go check out the rest of the book and see if she got everything else right.

Oh, no! All our secrets!

Here are all the reasons it's better to watch us birds than other critters!
1. More exciting than slugs!
2. More varieties than squirrels!
3. Less dangerous than grizzly bears!
You're not going to let him eat that right here on the opening page, are you? He'll gross everyone out!
Just warning you... roadkill ahead! Hope you're not squeamish!
What's THAT supposed to mean? Eating dead stuff is natural and beautiful.
C'mon, you guys, why can't you be nice and cute and quiet like these little guys on the other page?

This is a book about one of my favorite hobbies: bird-watching (and bird drawing, too!).

But I should warn you right up front, I'm not a professor of ornithology (which is the fancy name for "study of birds") or anything like that. I'm not an expert bird-watcher — not a single pair of my binoculars even works properly! I just really love birds.

I wasn't always a bird-watcher, but several years ago, I thought it would be nice to keep a nature sketchbook. When I sat outside to draw trees and rocks and flowers, I couldn't help but begin to notice lots of birds, some I knew and some I didn't, flitting around the edges of my drawings.

Had they been there all along, and I just hadn't been paying attention?

I couldn't stop watching them, and before I knew it, I was hooked.

Oh, I know what you're thinking....

Bird-watching is NOT boring! Is a hawk swooping down to gobble a mouse boring? Of course not. And how about crows getting into your neighbor's garbage? Also not boring . . . Those birds are really smart! (OK, you should probably go shoo them away. . . .)

Birds are, by far, the easiest-to-see of all wild creatures. No matter how small your corner of the world, there will be some birds in it. You might be amazed at just how thrilling it can be to see new birds, find out about them, and learn their names!

The point is . . . spending time outside observing life and drawing in a sketchbook can help you to see the world in a whole new way. You've always known that the birds and the trees and the insects and the rocks were there . . . but when you take the time to sit and patiently draw them, you do more than see them: you experience them. You feel yourself more connected to the natural world, more at home in it.

Some people think that nature is something experienced by *other* people—people who live out in the country. But no matter where you live, you are a part of the natural world, just as the birds and other creatures are. Your thoughts, feelings, and observations about nature are just as valid as anyone else's. You're the only one who can keep track of your specific experiences, so keep your sketchbook with you, write things down, and draw pictures. It's important.

A Great Place to Start

You don't have to go anywhere fancy to watch birds! No matter where you live, chances are, there's a lot more going on in your yard or on your street than you suspect.

What kinds of places are within walking distance of your house? Is there an old barn near you? It could be home to swifts, swallows, or maybe even a Barn Owl! If you're lucky enough to live near a marshy pond, keep your eyes open for Pied-billed Grebes, Great Blue Herons, and Red-winged Blackbirds. Anywhere that's a little different may have different birds!

Wing tip

Look in places where you usually don't, like low, under bushes, or high up, in the top branches of trees. Look *when* you usually don't, too . . . like early in the morning or just before dusk. You may find you don't know your own yard or your own street nearly as well as you thought you did!

Yeah, well, that's great for people with yards! What about people like me? How can I be a bird-watcher in the city, when all I can see out of my window is that one crummy tree there with little brown birds in it?
Well, let's start with those little brown birds. Do you know all there is to know about them? Are they finches or sparrows? Do you know which are the boys and which are the girls?
Do you know what they eat, where they live, if they stay all winter? Have you seen any babies? What sorts of noises do they make?
Are those pesky birds pooping on my windowsill again?

You may not have a yard, but you do have the sky. Look up! Many hawks, falcons, and even owls make their homes in the city.

City birds are tough and adaptive—meaning they make do with what they find. Little birds like pigeons and sparrows eat what they find on the streets; birds of prey hunt *them* from high perches atop buildings.

City birds aren't picky about where they live, either! Look closely and you may see a Mourning Dove nesting in an old pot on a terrace, an American Kestrel raising its babies behind a gargoyle, or sparrows and starlings taking up residence in any empty spot they can find.

A Northern Mockingbird may be found singing in any high spot.

Starlings

Here is a hawk zeroing in on her prey.

No one likes pigeons, but they are clever and resourceful!

The House Sparrow is probably the #1 most common city bird!

You might see the House Finch. The male has a rosy red breast.

What is that racket?

LAW OFFICE 871

So there you are, out behind your house or somewhere on your street, sitting in a quiet spot with your sketchbook, patiently waiting for the birds to show themselves. But once they turn up, what should you do?

The most important thing is to keep quiet and pay attention. Once you've had a chance to look closely, use sketches and little notes to yourself to keep a record in your notebook of the birds you see.

Try to sketch while keeping your eyes on the bird as much as you can. This takes practice, but it's so worth doing. Don't worry about how "good" your picture is—the act of drawing is valuable no matter what the result looks like, because when we draw, we look extra, extra hard, and that helps us focus our attention. There's so much to pay attention to—shape, color, sound, and more! So let's take each aspect one at a time.

A Rainbow of Color

We crows and ravens will be good and stay out of the color chart, as we are totally sharp super-black...

Lots of birds, like us guys here, have nice red decorations!

Red-headed Woodpecker

Red-winged Blackbird

Rose-breasted Grosbeak

Common Redpoll

Orange means one thing... orioles! Did you know we're related to blackbirds?

Hooded Oriole

Baltimore Oriole

Yellow Warbler

Eastern Meadowlark

Western Meadowlark

Blue-winged Warbler

Prothonotary Warbler

Unlike some other "black" birds I know, who insist on wearing ridiculous disco outfits!

Yellow-headed Blackbird

Black-billed Magpie

Green Jay

Lewis's Woodpecker

Steller's Jay

He's just jealous!

Tree Swallow

European Starling

I'm covered with colorful speckles... like stars!

Blue Jay

Pinyon Jay

Great-tailed Grackle

We grackles, magpies, and starlings look black from a distance, but our feathers are iridescent, showing shiny metallic colors up close.

'Cuz I'm the STARling. Get it? Clever, huh?

Purple Martin

Look Closely

Color can be a great way to identify birds. Even if you don't get a good look at a bird, a quick flash of red might be enough to tell you that you may have spotted a cardinal. Just remember that colors can look different in different light, especially in the late afternoon or evening, or if the bird is in deep shade. Also, note that sometimes male and female birds don't look alike — males are often brighter.

Don't forget black and white!

Black-footed Albatross

Audubon's Shearwater

Magnificent Frigatebird

Northern Gannet

California Gull

Brandt's Cormorant

Common Tern

Black Skimmer

White-tailed Tropicbird

Atlantic Puffin

I drew all these birds together to make a nice picture, but many of these birds, like the Puffins and the Tropicbird, don't really live even remotely near each other.

Common Eider

Western Grebe

Surf Scoter

Common Murre

Black Scoter

Common Loon

Bufflehead

Be a birdbrain

It isn't a coincidence that so many seabirds are gray or blackish on top and lighter below. This coloration works to their advantage, helping to hide them from the fish they're hunting and from other birds. (Many seabirds, like the Magnificent Frigatebird, are notorious for sneaking up and trying to steal one another's food. In fact, Frigatebirds are named after the type of ships pirates used!)

And then there's BROWN, too!

Birds will show you a whole world of brown! Look closely and you will soon be a connoisseur of this color. Study our bird color wheel and see how brown can be almost black . . . dark like tree bark or mottled like leaves . . . lovely russety-red or almost pink . . . golden like autumn grass . . . dusty and gray and plain as a mouse . . . or pale as sand . . .

Oh, look at all the poor dears, the color of dirt! So sad for them!

Be a birdbrain

Why do you think so many birds are so many different kinds of brown, with all manners of streaks and spots? Can you think of any advantages for brown birds?

No one here but us moldy leaves!

13

Shapes Are Clues

Many birds have characteristic silhouettes, whether perching on a wire, sitting on the water, or flying. How many of these shapes have you seen?

Yellow Warbler

House Wren

Song Sparrow

Barn Swallow

Tree Swallow

Eastern Kingbird

Eastern Phoebe

Mourning Dove

Rock Dove (Pigeon)

Belted Kingfisher

Red-tailed Hawk

The Great Blue Heron flies in an unhurried, gentlemanly manner, neck neatly folded.

Kingfisher hovering

Downy Woodpecker

Great Blue Heron

Ibises fly with necks out!

Double-crested Cormorant

Ospreys hover to hunt. You might see one carrying a fish!

Hairy Woodpecker

White Ibis

Black-crowned Night Heron (neck folded)

Cormorants and Anhingas both stand with their wings spread to dry.

Cormorants swim low in the water.

Mute Swan (More famous swan shape)

The Anhinga swims even lower; it looks like a snake sticking up.

Tundra Swan

The Turkey Vulture is famous for flying in a V shape, called a dihedral.

American Crow

People say "as the crow flies" because crows fly fast and straight.

Here is a Herring Gull, a typical seagull.

The Common Raven also flies as if she has important business to get to.

Terns are a bit pointier.

Common Tern

The Mourning Dove, like all pigeons and doves, is also a strong, fast flier.

Nighthawks and Chimney Swifts fly erratically, which means this way and that.

Flickers fly in a great swoopy up-and-down way! This is called undulating flight.

A flock of Brown Pelicans flies as though they are being pulled along on a string. They are lovely to watch.

Hummingbirds zip around like tiny manic helicopters!

Look Closely

Try to capture the general shape of a bird in your sketchbook, and take note of how it flies: Is its flight fast and powerful or weak and clumsy? Is the bird agile? Does it dart about gracefully? Does it dive? Think about the shape of its body, and especially the shape of its wings. Does the shape of its wings have anything to do with how it flies?

15

Take note of the general shape of the bird you're looking at. Is it . . .

round and
plump?

short and
sturdy?

thin and
sneaky?

short-legged and
long necked?

Then consider all those other interestingly shaped important bird parts, like bills. Is the
bird's bill . . .

a straight,
strong chisel?

thin, delicate
tweezers?

a tearing
hook?

a scoopy
shovel?

What about feet? What kind of feet does the bird you're looking at have? Are they . . .

big, scary
clawed feet?

flipper feet?

climbing feet?

little gripping,
perching feet?

strong walkin'
feet?

Some birds sport fanciful hairdos and cool little hats (field guides call 'em crests).

The Pileated Woodpecker wears a jaunty cap!

The Wood Duck is looking fine!

The Northern Cardinal wears a little bishop's miter.

We're like the Incredible Hulks of the avian world!

Yeah! You see the crests up, you gonna get messed up!

Some crests are small and secret, like those of the Orange-crowned Warbler and Ruby-crowned Kinglet, and only shown when the bird is feeling aggressive.

Many of these crests are quite eye-catching!

It's called a PLUME. I assure you, it's QUITE NOBLE.

Some quails wear a neat little deely-bopper kind of hat.

The Greater Roadrunner's crest adds to his rakish good looks.

The Great Horned Owl has "horns" that are quite great.

Why is he looking at me like that?

The Horned Lark has horns that are quite wee.

Anything else interesting? Tails, perhaps? Take note!

Um, it's not my tail.

I just have extra-long wing feathers.

Cranes wear bustles, like old-timey ladies.

Well, dearie, it LOOKS like a tail!

Hey, lady, watch out for your bustle!

Scissor-tailed Flycatcher

These are some good tails, but mine is, you know... GREAT.

Just sayin'.

Great-tailed Grackle

What Are They Up To?

Learning about birds goes far beyond noticing what they look like. When we watch birds closely—when we see how they move, eat, communicate, build their nests—this is called observing their behavior, and it's what scientists do!

You have probably done a bit of this already. Imagine it is very early morning, and there are birds in your yard. They are hopping a bit, maybe running around, stopping, cocking their heads, and pulling up worms. Do you know who they are?

You may not be able to see them very clearly, but the way they're acting can give you some clues. Birds are predictable—you won't catch an eagle hopping around on your lawn, pulling up worms! Those birds in your yard are exhibiting classic robin behavior.

I know who those guys are— I see them every day!

This is why you shouldn't feel bad if you're not able to get out and see many new birds. If you get to know your most familiar neighbors really, really well, then you will be all the more ready to notice something different should anyone new happen by. (This is one of the most important things I can tell you.)

19

When you're paying attention to a bird's behavior, one of the most obvious things you'll notice is who it spends its time with. The robin is a social bird—he likes to be with others of his same kind, which is called being gregarious. For social birds like this, there can be safety in numbers, as well as advantages in locating and foraging for food.

Chickadees are also social birds who enjoy the company of their close relatives. (These groups are called mixed flocks.)

Crows roost together by the hundreds.

Cliff Swallows build their own mud apartment houses!

But not all birds are like that! Some are much more territorial, preferring to be the only ones on the block.

You might think wrens are little and cute, but they're really tough guys.

Mockingbirds are pretty aggressive, too!

Hawks are mostly solitary, but some will occasionally hunt with their mates or in other small family groups.

Speaking of hawks, here is a behavior you might see sometime. It is called mobbing, and it's when little birds band together to drive a bigger bird—like a hawk—out of town!

Here are a few other behaviors you might be able to see. . . .

Male pigeons strut about with their feathers fluffed out. This is called displaying, and it's how they attract a mate.

Birds in springtime gather grasses, twigs, and moss for nest building.

A Killdeer will pretend to have a broken wing to lure a predator away from her nest.

Bird behavior is a fascinating subject to read about! Every species has its own way of doing things—gathering food, attracting a mate, building a nest (or not, like those vultures on the right). Learn about their lives, and your understanding of birds will be all the richer.

Note the Fine Details

As we saw on the rainbow page, very few birds are one solid color . . . yes, except for you, Mr. Crow, and Mr. Raven, and Mr. Purple Martin! Pretty much everyone else has varying shades of one color, or several colors, or a pattern of some sort. Even our plainest birds usually have a few markings . . . a little something special about their appearance so that they can recognize one another as members of their species. These are called field marks, and you can think of them as decorations, if you'd like!

Foot note

Many field marks, like the Flicker's mustache, are worn by the male birds only. Out of the marks shown here, only those of the Sandwich Tern and the Yellow-rumped Warbler are worn by both sexes.

Though some field marks, like the Wood Duck's, are quite easy to see, you might have to look a little harder for the subtler ones. The more you practice, the more you will begin to see the differences among all those little brown birds.

bright eye stripe

white corners on tail

Bewick's Wren

Yeah, like us little brown wrens here! You might think we all look alike, but really, we don't!

bright-white eyebrow

white streaks

Marsh Wren

Yeah! For example, I'm the only one here with cool shoulder stripes!

You can tell us apart by our field marks, like my eyebrow and the dark bars on my tummy...

Hey, I do SO have field marks!

Winter Wren

...or by our lack of field marks, like poor House Wren here!

House Wren

Well, so my bars aren't as dark as yours. OK, OK... and it's true, I don't have much of an eyebrow, but still...

Yeah, let's show 'em!

Hey, Field Sparrow! That kid's having trouble "identifying" us. Should we invite him to our fashion show?

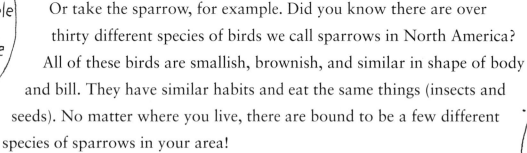

Or take the sparrow, for example. Did you know there are over thirty different species of birds we call sparrows in North America? All of these birds are smallish, brownish, and similar in shape of body and bill. They have similar habits and eat the same things (insects and seeds). No matter where you live, there are bound to be a few different species of sparrows in your area!

To tell them apart, you need to look at their field marks very carefully.

By the way, it's TREE SPARROW. I have a spot, too, y'know!

MODERN SPARROW
Hey, did I hear someone say they can't tell us apart? Maybe our fashion show will help!
How can people think we look alike? Really, now!
Yes! Imagine mistaking your big ol' football helmet for my sleek li'l Italian-style racing cap! Funny!
FOOTBALL HELMET?
And over here we have Chipping Sparrow in a clever red cap and very distinct white eyebrows!
American Tree Sparrow also sports a red cap and notched tail, and adds a stylish stick pin!
Starting us off today is Song Sparrow, working a rather severe look with the bold chest spot and streaking she is famous for...
Good thing you wore the bib. The bugs they're serving are pretty messy.
Oh, yeah, I always wear it to these things.
I could totally rock that look!
I just don't think I could pull that off!
But on her, it works!

Feathers 'n' Such

As we saw in the previous section, you can tell birds apart by their little details. But here's where things can get a bit complicated: a bird doesn't always look the same from one year to the next, or from one season to the next.

Think about people . . . and all the changes they go through as they grow up. Most people wear different clothes, depending on what life stage they're in. (Unless they're my friend Carl.)

Birds change outfits, too! Only with them, it's feathers. This is called plumage.

Once they grow up, many birds keep the same look for the rest of their lives.

The male is often brighter than the female. Sometimes a lot brighter . . .

and sometimes just a little bit.

In a few pairs, the male and female don't appear to be the same species!

And in others, the sexes look exactly the same.

Many other birds wear a flashier look in spring and summer, called breeding plumage.

This brighter look helps to attract a mate, and it can be a whole new colorful outfit, like the male Scarlet Tanager's . . .

. . . or just a few fanciful plumes, like these Double-crested Cormorants have.

Listen Closely

When you go out to look at birds, make sure you listen to them, too! Their singing can be lovely to hear, of course, but they sing to communicate with one another, not just to sound pretty. Think of all the ways birds use sound.

HEY! THIS IS MY BRANCH!

And so's this one, so KEEP OFF!

I'm a catch! I know a lot of songs, and I sing 'em all pretty nice!

Oh, ladies... listen to me!

Here's a little ditty I learned from dear ol' dad....

They sing to establish their territory and to advertise themselves to a potential mate.

Hi! I'm over here!

I'm over here!

Birds call to keep in touch with one another, and to warn one another of danger. Maybe they're talking to you, too!

Hand over the sandwich, ma'am.

CAT!

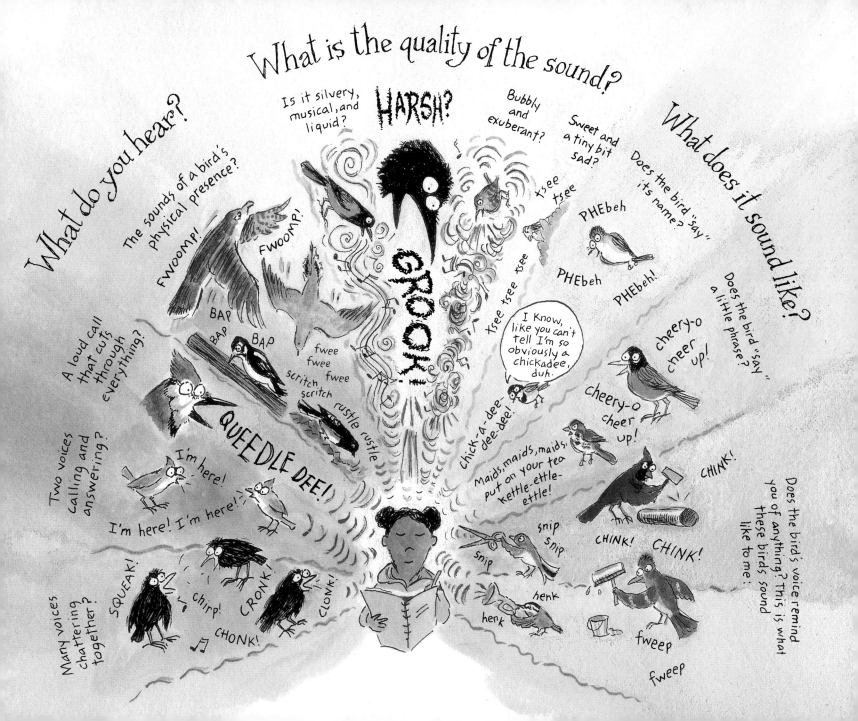

Time for a Field Guide!

A Field Guide to the Birds of Whidbey Island

Now that you're becoming more aware of all the birds in your area, and you're noticing all their various shapes and colors and habits and songs . . . is it occurring to you that there are a lot more birds around than you thought? Maybe you've seen some new ones and you'd like to learn their names . . . but how can you do that? You could ask a local bird-watcher, if you know one. Or you could crack open a field guide!

Every Single Bird Who Lives On or Has Ever Visited This Continent

Field guides are great to have. They'll tell you everything you need to know about a bird and help you make sense of all your observations. Your local library probably has a few to look at. Some field guides might make you feel overwhelmed at first; you might want to start with a beginner's guide or one with birds more specific to your area.

The Beginner's Book of Backyard Birds

Most are arranged by families, which will help you to narrow down what bird it is that you are trying to identify.

Here's a whole bunch of birds that look kind of like the one I saw... It was probably a sparrow.

Or was it a warbler? Whoa...There's TONS of them!

Hey... "Worm-eating Warbler!" That's funny.

Most field guides will give both common and scientific names.

There will be a physical description, with field marks to look for and facts about voice, behaviors, diet, and nesting habits . . . all that good stuff!

Chipping Sparrow
Spizella passerina

Red cap

White wing bars

Notched tail

Known for his red cap, notched tail, and call of rapidly trilled "chip" notes. Little flocks of them are commonly found in yards, shrubbery, fields, and open woodlands. Diet consists of insects in summer and grass and weeds in winter. Nest is a finely woven cup of grasses and hair, found 25 feet up in a tree.

Juvenile

First winter

Winter non-breeding

A good guide will show if there are various plumages, and tell you if the male and female don't look alike.

Most will have range maps showing where the bird is found and where it goes if it migrates.

So... who was that cute little guy I saw on the lawn?

Hmm... my bird kind of looks like a Seaside Sparrow. Wait a minute, I live in Iowa, so that seems unlikely....

Brewer's Sparrow? Nah... says here they live in mountain meadows, so that's also unlikely. Ditto for Sage Sparrow, I suppose...

Keep trying, Kid!

Wing tip

If you buy a field guide, take it with you when you go out to look at birds! But try not to waste time looking up birds in a book when the actual birds are right in front of you — you don't want anything to distract you from watching the real birds carefully, and there'll be plenty of time to look them up in your field guide after they've flown away!

The Power of Observation

Let's take a look now at two very distinct birds. We'll compare their various attributes and see all the ways they are different from each other—and what those differences mean to the birds.

A bird looks the way it does for a reason. You can often figure out what—or who!—a bird eats and how it spends its time by paying attention to what it looks like.

One of the best places to look for birds whose features are adapted to their environment is by the water. It's clear that these birds are fish eaters!

Pelicans scoop fish out of the water with their pouches!

I stab at thee!

Cormorants can swallow fish and eels thicker than their own throats!

The Black Skimmer skims fish right from the water's surface.

Herons wade into the water with their long legs, then wait patiently and strike with their daggerlike bills!

On the other hand, a cardinal's no fisherman . . .
you can tell just by looking at him.

What's THAT?

Help!

This is NOT working!

Oh yes . . . very funny, ha ha. Who wants to eat a dumb squid anyway?

First of all, fish would find that bright red color alarming!

The cardinal has pointy little perching feet, no good for swimming!

And even if he caught a fish, he could never hold on to it with that stumpy, chunky bill of his!

Just as we saw with the various seabirds, birds generally eat what they are best adapted to eat. Each bird has developed specialized "tools"—bills and feet—that help it get its favorite foods.

Some thrashers' bills are like pickaxes for digging in hard soil for bugs.

Purple Gallinules have super-long toes for walking on floating vegetation.

Owls and hawks kill with their powerful feet and sharp talons.

Much better than squid!

Cardinals' thick, strong bills are perfect for cracking nuts and seeds.

Don't forget my chiselly bill and my long, sticky bug-grabbing tongue!

Those dumb bugs don't stand a chance!

Wrens have thin, curved bills for extracting insects from crevices.

Woodpeckers' feet are specially adapted for climbing and clinging to vertical surfaces. Even their tails help them balance as they climb.

All parrots are quite adept at using their feet like hands!

Who are the most highly specialized birds of all? They may well be vultures and condors! Although many people find them . . . uh . . . a little icky and creepy, due to their somewhat unpleasant habits, they have some extremely efficient adaptations for eating carrion (that means dead stuff).

These birds help to keep the earth clean by eating things no other bird will eat . . . and that's not icky or creepy at all! In fact, maybe there's something beautiful about it.

"Creepy"?

Strong hooked bill for tearing flesh

Big strong wings for endless soaring in search of food

The bird's small head can be thrust deep into carcasses; its naked skin is easier to keep clean than feathers.

Yep... that's been there a week now! You know I like a bit of carrion now and again, but I have my limits! It's all yours, buddy!

Mmph— yep, that was a stinky one, all right! Smelled it a mile away.

Their stomachs are able to digest REALLY putrid meat filled with noxious microbes.

Turkey vultures can locate food by smell!

Be a birdbrain

When you look at a bird, keep in mind all the things we have studied: size, shape, color, pattern, way of moving. Can you see how it's equipped to make its living? Can you make predictions about what it eats and how it gets that meal?

Where Birds Are At: Habitat

If you visit different parts of your town, you may notice that the birds in your yard are different from the ones down the street, or in the supermarket parking lot, or at the soccer field, or wherever. That's because every bird has a certain environment that suits it best for how it lives and what it eats. This environment is called a habitat. Consider the Roadrunner:

She can build her nest in a cactus!

Her body is extremely efficient, so she doesn't need much water.

Mmmm! I do love a juicy smashed-up snake!

Her drab, mottled plumage helps her to blend in with her dry, dusty surroundings.

Her long legs and big strong feet are ideal for running quickly over hard, open terrain.

As you can see, the desert is a good place for a Roadrunner! Here are some other birds who live in very specific places. . . .

Kingfishers nest in long tunnels they dig into riverbanks. They also need the river for fishing.

The river can't be TOO fast, or TOO shallow, or TOO deep.

It has to be perfect. Not that I'm picky.

The American Dipper needs a fast-moving, somewhat shallow stream for foraging.

Here I am, the noble Spruce Grouse, in a spruce grove, eatin' some spruce needles.

Yep yep yep.

The Spruce Grouse . . . enough said.

Birds are thought to be "successful" if they can adapt to living in all sorts of places and can eat what they find in those places.

Other birds' diets are much more tied to their habitat, and so they are much less flexible and, unfortunately, more likely to be endangered.

Both the Greater and Lesser Prairie Chickens need open prairies for food and nesting.

The Snail Kite's curved bill is perfect for eating apple snails, which are found in the marshlands of Florida.

Home in the Range

Although you can see quite a variety of birds by seeking out different habitats near where you live, you generally need to be within a bird's range—the geographical area in which it is typically found—to see it.

Because I live in New England...

I must face facts and accept that I will not see a flamingo flying over my house, or a California Quail trotting through my yard, or a penguin swimming at the beach.

It's sad, but...

I will console myself with the thought that I could see an Atlantic Puffin, if I wanted!

I mean, I would have to drive a long way and then take a ferry ride... but still, I could!

Remember Ms. Roadrunner? Her range is strictly southern . . . from California to Arkansas and Louisiana, and down into Mexico. She thrives in dry, open habitats like desert and grasslands. The Southwest is her range because that's where she finds her required food and shelter.

Well, I should hope they would remember me! I was just on the last page. Good grief.

A bird who is less dependent on a specific habitat may well have a larger range, like our fine, charming friend, the ubiquitous European Starling, who is found throughout the U.S. and Canada, visible just about anywhere there are people.

Probably just about everyone in North America has seen a starling . . . but what about a few of these other very common birds, who also have very large ranges?

If you have a family vacation coming up, you might get a chance to see birds that don't live in your area! (Remember to always bring your sketchbook and drawing materials on trips!) Zoos, aquariums, and natural history museums can also be great places to learn about birds you might not otherwise see.

North America is a very large continent!

And it's very geographically diverse. As many as 800 species of birds may call it home at any given time (though some are just passin' through), and some of them have very specific habitats and therefore very specific ranges. This map shows a few!

Do birds read our silly maps? No! Their ranges change all the time, sometimes expanding, like that of the Cardinal, and sometimes shrinking, like that of the Snail Kite, which is now endangered in the U.S.

41

To You It's Vacation; to Us It's Migration!

Have you ever noticed that the birds you see in summer may not be the same ones you see in winter? Many birds migrate, traveling a lot (or just a little) to find better weather, more food, or their traditional breeding grounds. If you live in the northern part of the United States (like me), you've probably noticed there are fewer birds around in winter. But because most birds fly south, there are a few kinds of birds I actually see more of in the winter, like Dark-eyed Juncos. They migrate from Canada to Massachusetts . . . because even though it's wintry and cold where I am, it's still warmer than it is in Canada!

Most field guides will have maps with a key showing different information like this:

- ■ Summer or breeding range
- □ Winter range
- ⬚ Migration range
- ▨ Year-round range
- ⊙ "Rare" or "accidental" sightings

Rare sightings can happen when a bird gets blown off course. Maybe an albatross will pop up in your yard someday! You never know. . . .

Some birds make migratory trips of almost unbelievable lengths. Don't be too quick to dismiss that little brown sparrow—she could be resting up from an amazing journey!

The Arctic Terns are a very dramatic example— they may fly 31,000 miles every year!

Other birds, like these puffins, migrate just a bit.

Arctic Terns spend the summer up here... then fly all the way down to Antarctica... where they spend the winter (the Antarctic summer)... then fly all the way back again!

Be a birdbrain

Think about the birds you see around you in all the seasons. Who's there in spring, making nests? Are you part of their breeding range? Maybe you see some birds for only a few days in the fall because you're a stop on their migration route. And what about winter — who stays, and who goes? If it's warm where you are, do you get an influx of winter residents?

When scientists classify life-forms, they group them together in a series of categories. These groups start off very large and general, then are organized into smaller and smaller subgroups as the life-forms inside them become more and more alike by scientific standards.

Scientists estimate there may be as many as 20 million different life-forms on Earth (most are molds, bacteria, and insects . . . but still!), and they've only officially classified about a million and a half of them! With such an amazing variety of life, you can see how important it is for scientists to have a way to keep track of everything!

Even though he's very closely related to the other birds in his genus, Lincoln's Sparrow and Swamp Sparrow, the Song Sparrow is still very much his own species. He looks like a Song Sparrow, sings Song Sparrow songs, has a lady Song Sparrow for his mate, and raises baby Song Sparrows. That's what it means to be *Melospiza melodia,* to use his scientific name.

– AHEM! – Uh, one might also say "Linnaean name," because I, Carolus Linnaeus, had the totally cool idea to name all living things this way.

Y'see, back in the 1700s, scientists were naming critters all willy-nilly, and it was a big mess. So I said, "Dudes, this is nuts. From now on, let's have names be two words denoting genus and species, and it will be totally official and totally awesome!"

Thanks, Mr. L.! Great idea! Not that we birds need those big fancy names or anything....We know they're just for you humans!

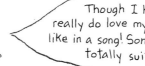

Though I have to say, I really do love my name, Melodia...melody... like in a song! Song Sparrow! Get it? It totally suits me, right?

It's fun when birds' names tell little stories about them! Here are a few more. . . .

The Wood Duck's Latin name, Aix sponsa, means "Duck who is betrothed."

The Northern Mockingbird's Latin name, Mimus polyglottus, means "many-tongued mimic."

The Dark-eyed Junco's Latin name, Junco hyemalis, means "Junco of the winter."

And here are a few easy scientific names for you to learn!

Well, here we are, at the end of everything I have room to tell you! I hope this book has helped to start you on your way to watching and drawing birds . . . and I hope that experiencing the natural world and keeping a sketchbook will bring you great joy for all the years of your life, too!

You can be any kind of bird-watcher you want to be—you might spend your life searching for rare birds, or you might just like to check out your local sparrows every now and then. It's up to you!

Always remember that you are part of this world . . .
so grab your faithful sketchbook, get out there,
and take a look around!

Bibliography

This book grew from my own observations and experiences sketching birds, but I read many books along the way to help me with my drawing and writing.

Speech bubble: "Wait a minute— I'm supposed to eat worms?"

How to Know the Birds: An Introduction to Bird Recognition by Roger Tory Peterson. Boston: Houghton Mifflin, 1962.
    Everyone interested in bird-watching should own this book.
There isn't a friendlier, more charming introduction anywhere.
The writing is an absolute delight, and the pictures are so helpful.
Don't ask me why I thought there was anything else to add!

Speech bubble: "Should've added some emus."

The Sibley Guide to Bird Life and Behavior, illustrated by David Sibley. New York: Knopf, 2001.
    This book is stuffed to the brim with facts and beautiful pictures. It was indispensable to me.

Speech bubble: "Mr. Sibley's drawings are much nicer than the ones in this book—"

Speech bubble: "he actually draws the right number of toes!"

Birdsong: A Natural History by Don Stap. New York: Scribner, 2005.
    This wonderful book explains how and why birds sing.

Naming Nature: The Clash Between Instinct and Science by Carol Kaesuk Yoon. New York: Norton, 2009.
    I loved learning about the way all life-forms are related, and why it's important.

The Birds Around Us, edited by Alice Mace. San Francisco: Ortho Books, 1986.
    The chapter "Changes Through Time" by Kimball L. Garrett taught me about the whole flamingo-duck-heron business.

And I couldn't have drawn all my pictures, both the funny and serious ones, without consulting field guides! The ones I used the most were:

Field Guide to the Birds of North America by the National Geographic Society. Washington, D.C.: National Geographic, 1999.
    This book has the loveliest pictures.

Speech bubble: "I was the first bird she looked up!"

Speech bubble: "That's why she has a special place in her heart for us starlings!"

The Sibley Guide to Birds by David Allen Sibley. New York: Knopf, 2000.
    Again, I would be lost without Sibley! I went through this book so much, the cover fell off!

Peterson First Guide to Birds of North America by Roger Tory Peterson. Boston: Houghton Mifflin, 1986.
    This is the field guide that truly got me started.

Birds: A Guide to Familiar American Birds by Herbert S. Zim and Ira N. Gabrielson, New York: Golden, 1987.
    You can learn a lot from these little Golden Guides!

The website I consulted most often was the Cornell Lab of Ornithology's, at www.allaboutbirds.org. I used this when I wanted up-to-the-minute information about names, habitats, endangered status, that sort of thing. You can listen to birdsongs and watch videos, too!

Index

Hey, if you're ever in Phoenix, look me up!

I'll look you up right now... in the index!

I always thought it was "morning dove".

Now I feel sad!

I see we sparrows are very well represented...

'cause we RULE! We're way better than those silly warblers!

Only TWO pages for my magnificence? That does not seem right.

Shoot!

EIGHT pages, buddy! Just sayin'!

Hrumph!

Some Thoughts about Bird Drawing

Drawing birds is a lot of fun, but it isn't always easy at first! The #1 bit of advice I can give you is PRACTICE, and be patient. You'll get the hang of it! And #2, try to find birds who will sit still for you! Now get comfortable, and first think about SHAPE....

Getting the shape right is half the battle!

I LOVE ♡ Quails!

C'mon! This tail is not yet great!

Laughing Gulls have a cool triangular shape like a paper hat on the water.

Gulls are excellent drawing subjects.

Ooh, they hate when their dresses blow up!

Ever see a look of such utter indignation?

Drawing books often say, "start with an oval"... pretty good advice, really!

Ducks are such a nice shape to draw.

I have drawn many of these guys in my time.

I cannot stress enough: PRACTICE drawing the birds you see all the time. Like, say... robins! Do you really know them, well enough to draw them?

Are the wings held up or down?

How long is that tail?

How do those legs fit into the body?

What color are those legs?

I like to give them mad faces.

Crows, grackles, and starlings are the best!

Because they're black, they're all about shape. No worries about details!